W9-BGG-389

A QUICK GUIDE TO

Boosting English Acquisition
in Choice Time
K–2

Other Books in the Workshop Help Desk Series

A Quick Guide to
Reaching Struggling Writers, K–5
M. COLLEEN CRUZ

A Quick Guide to
Teaching Persuasive Writing, K–2
SARAH PICARD TAYLOR

A Quick Guide to
Making Your Teaching Stick, K–5
SHANNA SCHWARTZ

For more information about these and other titles,
visit www.firsthand.heinemann.com.

A QUICK GUIDE TO
Boosting English Acquisition in Choice Time
K–2

ALISON PORCELLI AND CHERYL TYLER

Workshop Help Desk Series

Edited by Lucy Calkins

with the Teachers College Reading and Writing Project

HEINEMANN

Portsmouth, NH

An imprint of Heinemann
361 Hanover Street
Portsmouth, NH 03801–3912
www.heinemann.com

Offices and agents throughout the world

© 2008 by Alison Porcelli and Cheryl Tyler

All rights reserved. No part of this book may be reproduced in any form or by
any electronic or mechanical means, including information storage and retrieval
systems, without permission in writing from the publisher, except by a reviewer,
who may quote brief passages in a review.

Library of Congress Cataloging-in-Publication Data
Porcelli, Alison.
 A quick guide to boosting English acquisition in choice time, K–2 / Alison Porcelli
and Cheryl Tyler.
    p. cm. — (Workshop help desk series)
 Includes bibliographical references.
 ISBN 13: 978–0–325–02615–2
 ISBN 10: 0–325–02615–7
 1. Language arts (Primary). 2. Reading (Primary). 3. English language—
Composition and exercises—Study and teaching (Primary). I. Tyler, Cheryl, 1947–
II. Title.
 LB1528.P675 2008
 372.6—dc22   2008030580

SERIES EDITOR: *Lucy Calkins and the Teachers College Reading and Writing Project*
EDITOR: *Kate Montgomery*
PRODUCTION: *Elizabeth Valway*
COVER DESIGN: *Jenny Jensen Greenleaf*
COVER PHOTO: *Comstock/Superstock*
INTERIOR DESIGN: *Jenny Jensen Greenleaf*
COMPOSITION: *House of Equations, Inc.*
MANUFACTURING: *Steve Bernier*

Printed in the United States of America on acid-free paper
12 11 10 09 08 VP 1 2 3 4 5

For Tom Porcelli, who always believes in me. Thank you for your love and endless encouragement.
—Alison

For Dylan, whose passion has been an inspiration to me.
—Cheryl

CONTENTS

ACKNOWLEDGMENTS

We must begin by thanking Lucy Calkins. Lucy's extraordinary vision and generosity have given us the opportunity to imagine unlimited possibilities for our students and for our own learning. It is that learning that has made this book possible. Thank you also to Laurie Pessah, who encouraged us at every step of the way, and to Kathleen Tolan, whose support was steadfast.

We'd like to thank Amanda Hartman for her wise advice and Shanna Schwartz for her encouragement and counsel. Kathy Collins' grace and humor have been an inspiration to us. Nekia Wise, Bonnie Rosen, Cara Biggane, Ali Scheler, Jenna Campbell, Heather Pearson, and Michelle McKenzie are brilliant teachers who understood the importance of this work and enthusiastically embraced it in their classrooms. We have learned so much from them. Audra Robb, Julia Mooney, Jen Serravallo, Gravity Goldberg, Stacey Fell-Eisenkraft, and Anne Taranto took time from their busy lives to read the manuscript and provide us with enormously helpful feedback. Denise Capasso's magnificent photography makes the book come alive with our kids. Kate Montgomery saw the potential from the beginning.

Alison would also like to thank her colleagues at the Teachers College Reading and Writing Project. I am so proud to be a part of such an important organization. Thank you for making me who I am as a teacher today. Thanks especially to the primary staff developers: Meghan Barry, Christine Cook, Rebecca Cronin, Dahlia Dallal, Kim Ethun, Ian Fleischer, Gravity Goldberg, Amanda Hartman, Christine Holley, Monique Knight, Lauren Kolbeck, Christine Lagatta, Mara Lansky, Arin Lavinia, Jory Lieber, Natalie Louis, Jessica Martin, Marjorie Martinelli, Enid Martinez, Beth Moore, Kristi Mraz, Marika Paez, Hannah Schneewind, Shanna Schwartz, Karma Suttles, Sarah Picard Taylor, and Joe Yukish. Thank you also to the teachers in my choice time leadership group, especially Natalie Perez, Sara Lee, Lauren Ranani, Claudia Coia, and Lauren Ginsberg. I would like to thank the teachers, coaches, and administrators at the schools where I tried this work out, especially P.S. 277, P.S. 112, P.S. 376, and P.S. 49. I am thankful for the teachers, administrators, students, and parents at Guilderland Elementary School and Coman Hill Elementary School, where I began my teaching career— particularly Leslie Abel, who always encouraged me to write a book. Thank you to my very large family of Kilts's, Many's, Sangalli's, Kilpatrick's, and Porcelli's for your unconditional love. Thank you to my friends for cheering me on, especially K.E., G.L.A.C., H.N., and J.Z.L.

Cheryl would like to thank an extraordinary group of educators at P.S. 277 who work tirelessly every day to open the doors to endless possibilities for our English language learners: Adele Cammarata, whose wisdom sustains me every day; Laura Hauser, who sees only children's strengths; Nery Pedraza, who is unwavering in her belief of what our kids can accomplish; and Allyson Daley, who has moved the school in ways we could have never imagined.

Teachers College Reading and Writing Project has nourished me as a teacher and has been at the heart of creating my vision as a principal. It has been such a privilege to think and learn with the best and the brightest of our profession: thanks to Marjorie Martinelli, Arin Lavinia, Jen Serravallo, Joe Yukish, Linda Chen, Eve Litwack, Monique Lopez, Hannah Schneewind, Karma Suttles, Leah Mermelstein, Renee Dinnerstein, Rebecca Cronin, Mary Chiarella, and Carl Anderson. My leadership group paved the way for this important work with their insights and brave teaching.

Adele Schroeter is a principal and friend who is passionate about the possibilities of choice time workshop and supported this work in many ways. Dan Feigelson was an important sounding board. Lucy Malka is always ready for a conversation that will push and challenge my thinking. And finally, my love and gratitude to Susan Felder, whose friendship and support never waver. Thank you!

English language learners (ELLs) flourish when they feel comfortable using English in a risk-free environment. In today's educational climate of standards, testing, and accountability, the sheer pace of instruction in most classrooms is enough to create a stressful environment. How important it is for young children, and especially young ELLs, to have a time in the school day when they can feel safe enough to approximate using English and meanwhile can work with zeal on collaborative projects that require lots of communication. In this book, we suggest that a choice time workshop can provide a rich and supportive opportunity within which ELLs can develop the language skills they need while also learning many of the constituent skills of strong reading and writing. In a choice time workshop, children can imagine, predict, envision, and problem solve, and they can do all this with support from each other, teachers, and literature.

We have written this book with the assumption that you already teach reading and writing as workshops and you have already found workshop teaching can provide powerful learning opportunities for children. We are also assuming that your class contains many ELLs. This book will help you provide your ELLs opportunities to make meaning through play. When children use blocks, construction paper, and improvisational drama to create alternate worlds and to inhabit those worlds, they're meanwhile drawn into a rich language curriculum. They use language to imagine and assess possibilities, to negotiate roles, to critique and revise work, and to assume roles. This language work is important for all youngsters and it is especially important for ELLs.

We believe passionately that young ELLs need to explore language through play. This belief was influenced by our experiences as early childhood teachers and as staff developers in primary classrooms brimming with ELLs. We were also inspired by the rock stars of education: Lev Vygotsky, Jean Piaget, Brian Cambourne, and Lucy Calkins.

In the first chapter, we suggest that choice time can be taught effectively within a workshop structure. In the second chapter, we emphasize the advantages that a choice time workshop can have for ELLs. The third and fourth chapters outline two units of study in choice time workshop and explore the notion of developing a curriculum for choice time.

The most rewarding part of writing this book was the collaborative aspect. Each chapter was truly written with a collective "we" and is infused with ideas and experiences from each of us.

CHAPTER ONE

Choice Time in a Workshop Structure

Anna, Cahle, Brianna, and Samuel, four ELLs at various stages of language proficiency, had just finished their dramatization of Paul Galdone's *Three Billy Goats Gruff* (1981) with a robust "Snip, snap, snout, and this tale's told out." They'd heard their teacher, Nery Pedraza, read this classroom favorite dozens of times. Their interpretation was impressive; in her role of the troll, Anna's face contorted as she clenched her fists and in a deep baritone roared, "Who's walking over my bridge?" As the group was cleaning the drama station and getting ready to gather on the rug, Anna paused and said to the others, "He always mad. He mean."

Cahle responded, "Let's do it again and be a nice troll." The children grinned and nodded in anticipation.

Russian psychologist Lev Vygotsky said, "In play, a child is always above his average age, above his daily behavior; in play, it is as though he were a head taller than himself" (Vygotsky 1978, 102). When Anna remarks about the trolls consistent meanness and Cahle suggests that the story could be reimagined, this time with a nice troll rather than a mean one, these children are allowing stories to be elastic. They are noticing patterns in a story and realizing that the story could have unfolded differently.

Teachers across America are increasingly being asked to develop teaching plans that are differentiated enough that every child in a class is able to function as an active, engaged learner. When many members of the class do not speak English, it is not always easy for teachers to know how to summon those children out of the margins of the classroom. Teachers who cannot speak a child's first language are not always sure how to reach the ELL, and equally important, they are not always sure how to help ELLs become socialized into the dynamics of a classroom. This book suggests that the choice time centers that were once a mainstay in so many early childhood classrooms can provide teachers with a developmentally appropriate way to engage all ELLs and to support their language development.

What, Exactly, Does the Phrase *Choice Time Workshop* Mean?

The phrase *choice time* refers to the portion of a day when children are allowed to work in areas of choice. Some early childhood educators are more blunt, calling this "play time," and some mask the prevalent activity, referring to this as "centers."

The label for this time is not important, but the fact that children have a chance to work (or play) with blocks, art materials, and drama is crucial. Increasingly, children do not have opportunities at home to make castles out of blocks or to cackle like a witch while casting a spell. Many children spend six hours a day watching television, and when they are not plugged into the television, children are plugged into the ipod, the computer, or the video game. "Our children," Bill Moyers has said, "are being raised by appliances."

Choice time is crucial, but this book aims to make a case not just for choice time but for a choice time *workshop*. This phrase—*choice time workshop*—implies not only that children are invited to play with blocks and construct art projects but also that this time adheres to the structures of workshop teaching. Lucy Calkins, the founding director of the Teachers College Reading and Writing Project at Columbia University, compares the structure of workshop teaching to that of a pottery class. In most pottery classes, the instructor starts out by convening the artists to share a point, to provide a demonstration. Then all the art students disperse to their various workstations and each resumes work on his or her pottery, picking up where he or she left off. As the pottery students work on their sculptures, they use not only the new technique that the teacher demonstrated that day but also other pottery techniques that they've been taught on previous days. The instructor, meanwhile, moves among the workers, observing, assessing, coaching, and sometimes convening small groups that need similar instruction. At the end of the workshop, the instructor might reconvene the group to share a technique that one or two members of the class tried that day.

Many teachers teach reading and writing within a structure not unlike a pottery workshop. Teachers begin reading and writing workshops with a short minilesson in which they demonstrate a particular teaching point, and then the students disperse to delve into their ongoing and important reading or writing work. As children read or write, they draw on what they have learned that day and on previous days. As children work, the teacher confers with individuals and leads small groups to provide responsive, differentiated instruction. The workshop closes with a brief teaching share—this is a time when the teacher highlights something that one person did during the workshop that could benefit all the others.

Teachers who teach choice time through a workshop structure find there are many advantages to such a structure, and those advantages are as important for children who are working with clay or blocks as for children who are working with written words and illustrations. Perhaps most importantly, workshop teaching allows children to work for long stretches of time, pursuing their own wonderful ideas. Years ago, Donald Graves described the elementary school curriculum as a "cha-cha" curriculum, with children spending five minutes on one thing, seven minutes on the next. "Take it out," the teacher says, and then says, "Put it away."

Workshops—whether reading workshops, writing workshops, or choice time workshops—are designed to provide learners with long chunks of time so that they have the opportunity to plan, to construct, to revise, and to share work. The nature of that work will be different depending on whether this is a choice time workshop, a writing workshop, or a reading workshop, but in all three instances, learners are given long stretches of time to carry on with some independence. In a choice time workshop, children stay in their center for at least that one day's workshop and eventually for several days. This is not a small accomplishment. Before structuring choice time into a workshop format, many of our students used to bounce from blocks to art to drama and back to blocks. For example, Matthew would start a painting in the art station and then leave his unfinished work while he ran to the block station to knock down a structure. By the time others heard the commotion in the block area and gathered to investigate, Matthew had already moved on to the game area. If Matthew were working within a choice time workshop, once he or his teacher had channeled him into one kind of exploration, Matthew would be expected to pursue that exploration for at least a day, if not for several days.

Although choice time workshops provide children with opportunities for extended independent work, these workshops also provide children with explicit instruction from a teacher who intervenes to demonstrate and scaffold skills that children need. These skills and strategies are then put to use on students' own important projects. All of this happens in a sea of talk. Children confer with a teacher, and they work in partnerships and small groups.

Many teachers wonder about the notion that children's work with blocks and drama be part of a structured instructional time. "Children have such a structured day already; can't we let their play be unstructured?" they often ask. This is a wise question, but ultimately, blocks, art, and drama provide these young children (and especially young ELLs) with such important learning opportunities that teachers imply can't miss out on the chance to teach into this important work. The following chart illustrates the structure of a typical choice time workshop:

Minilesson (5 minutes)
Minilessons in choice time workshops follow the same architecture as minilessons in reading and writing workshops. The teacher names and demonstrates one thing she hopes children learn to do as they work on their projects. The children receive scaffolded practice doing whatever the teacher has taught. Sometimes that practice involves a few minutes of work with a partner. Before children disperse at the end of the minilesson, the teacher restates what it is that she hopes children have learned.
Independent Work Time (25–35 minutes)
During work time, children work independently or collaborative work on a project the child authors or coauthors. Some children will have invented a project for themselves to pursue in art, others meanwhile will be making a project on blocks. Different stations allow children to represent their thinking in different ways and to draw on multiple sign systems to do so.
Teaching Share (3–5 minutes)
After the work time, children reconvene back at the carpet. Often the teacher highlights something that she saw in one of the stations that either further illustrates or extends her teaching point.

The Minilesson

In a writing workshop, one child might be writing about skating and another child, about a birthday party. The teacher, meanwhile, convenes the whole class to teach a minilesson that will be applicable to all the varied work that children are pursuing. Similarly, in the choice time workshop, a teacher needs to teach minilessons that pertain across the various domains. For example, the teacher might teach children about the value of planning, suggesting children do this whether they are making a house out of pipe cleaners or a spaceship out of a cardboard box. There are countless lessons that a teacher could teach that are equally applicable across the array of choice time centers. Teachers could teach children to talk to each other about their plans and, specifically, to monitor for sense while participating in these conversations by saying to each other, when necessary, "I don't understand what you are saying. Could you find another way to show me what you mean?" Teachers could teach children that whatever they are doing, they can always use books as a resource. Even children who cannot read conventionally can learn from many nonfiction sources because most of them contain lots of illustrations. These and other minilessons, then, can pertain across domains, so that block builders, artists, and dramatists all profit from the teacher's instruction.

In choice time workshops, minilessons are patterned after the lessons in *Units of Study for Primary Writing* (Calkins et al. 2003). In those minilessons, the teacher convenes children for about ten minutes. The first minute or two of the minilesson is a time to gather children's attention, to contextualize today's lesson, and to teach children a skill or a strategy that they can use many days on their ongoing work projects.

For example, I (Alison) recently began a minilesson by calling the children over to the carpet and saying to them, "Thinkers, during the reading workshop we have been learning that it helps if reading partners take a second to plan how our partnership reading time will go. Rather than diving right into reading, you have been having a quick conversation to plan. You not only plan how you'll read, you also plan how you'll work with another person. Planning is important not only before we read but also before we work with blocks or with an art project or with almost anything. Before you get started on almost anything, it helps to think, 'How will this work go?' and more specifically, to think, 'How will I work with other people on this?'"

"This means that before you get started working during choice time today and every day, you'll want to turn to others who will be working alongside you and ask, 'What do you want to work on?' Then, just like in reading workshop, you can decide what you'll do first so that you can work together on whatever you decide upon."

Turning to a student, I said, "So let's pretend that Brandon is in the block station with me. Before we start building, I am going to say to him, 'Let's plan how we will work together. What do you want to work on?' and after responding, he may ask me the same question. You'll see that we'll decide together how we will get started. Watch me."

Shifting into the demonstration portion of this minilesson, I invited Brandon up to help me teach and said, "Hi, Brandon. Let's plan. What do you want to work on today?"

Brandon replied, "Building a castle."

Then I whispered to Brandon that he might want to ask me, "What do you want to work on?" and he did just that.

I replied, "I want to build a dinosaur city." Then we talked through whether to start with one idea or the other and ended up deciding to start with Brandon's idea to build a castle.

Stepping back to help students reflect on that interaction, I said, "So did you see how Brandon and I asked each other what we wanted to work on, and when we had two good possibilities before us, we chose one as the starting point? You can do the same thing." This ended the teaching section of my minilesson.

Then, to give children a few minutes of practice with this, I instructed station partners to turn to each other and ask, "What do you want to work on today?" As children held these conversations, I circulated among them.

After a moment, I reconvened the class and highlighted what a couple of kids had said and then closed with a reminder: "So from now on, remember that when you are working with others, it is wise to plan and one important part of planning involves deciding how the two or three of you will work together. Who will do which jobs? You need to take time to plan what you will do first, then next."

Then I sent off members of one station and then another; children moved swiftly from the carpet area to their station so as to not waste any time.

Independent Work

In the block station during a choice time workshop, children might work together to build a car garage. Perhaps Anthony and Jason are trying to make the structure really tall, but it keeps falling down. The two boys work zealously, testing different alternatives for rebuilding and repairing the structure.

When they finally get the structure to stand, Anthony might make a sign with black marker, "kep up" (keep up), and then he might tape this sign to the structure, hoping in this way that no one will knock it down the next day.

A different section of the room might have been transformed into the drama station. The cluster of children in this station are pretending they are at a restaurant. One child is the waiter, another, the cook, and a third, is sitting at the telephone with a blank book in hand, furiously scribbling down phone orders.

In the art station, a big piece of butcher block paper is rolled out on the table. Children are working on different sections, painting what looks like a giant dinosaur.

This view of a choice time workshop will reveal that children are working (or perhaps the better word is *playing*) with engagement. Looking deeper, though, it is obvious that this is hardly a laissez-faire situation. The teacher is there, too, and she moves quickly from one station to another, listening in and intervening to coach learners to tackle more ambitious work.

When the teacher moves among learners in a choice time workshop, she's doing what teachers always do: observing, assessing, coaching, demonstrating, and extending. It is hard to overemphasize the importance of assessment. During choice time workshops, teachers have the chance to see children working in settings that may not, to the children, feel academic. How important it is for the teacher to collect language samples of ELLs' talk. How important it is, too, for teachers to serve as language models for ELLs, talking with kids about what they are doing and then giving them the language that surrounds their actions.

In choice time workshops, as in reading and writing workshops, independent work time is brought to a close by the teacher convening children for a brief share session. After hearing the signal that conveys the message "clean up," children put away their materials and gather in the meeting area for what is often referred to as a *teaching share* because the teacher often highlights an example of student work that could benefit the rest of the class in some way.

The Teaching Share

During one day's share session, the teacher might say to the entire class, "I want to tell you something special that I saw today. Mounaf had scissors that Jessica wanted. Rather than yelling and grabbing, she asked him in a helpful way, 'Can you share the scissors with me, please?' and he handed them to her. So we learned from Mounaf and Jessica that if someone has something you want, rather than yelling and grabbing, you can ask in helpful way. You could even add the reasons why you need that thing—Mounaf could have added,'I need them to cut out the stars for my crown.'" The teacher could then say, "Pretend your partner has some glue, and you want it. Pretend Partner One has the glue. Partner Two, for just a minute think about why you might need that glue . . . what might you be doing that requires glue? Now Partner Two, tell your partner what you'd like, and why. Be sure to add your reasons."

A Curriculum Made Up of Units of Study

In reading and writing workshops, although every day's reading or writing time is structured in a predictable fashion, the work that children pursue changes across the year. Teachers plan monthlong units of study, and those units help to steer and to inform the work that children do as readers and writers. For example, in a writing workshop, the teacher might plan that for one month, children will write narratives, and for another month, children will write persuasive letters. Similarly, teachers who lead choice time workshops find it is helpful to plan units of study for the entire year.

In some schools, teachers plan at least four and sometimes five or six units of study for their yearlong choice time workshop. This book focuses specifically on Units 1 and 2.

Unit 1: Planning and Pursuing Collaborative Projects

Unit 2: Story Play

Unit 3 and 4: Planning and Inventing Projects Based in Social Studies or Science

Unit 5 and 6: Planning and Inventing Interest-Based Projects

CHAPTER TWO

The Benefits of Choice Time Workshop for English Language Learners

One day during the second unit of study, Story Play, Jocelyn, Andrew, and Yesenia were building with the blocks. The three first-grade ELLs used four round blocks and two triangular blocks (for ears). Jocelyn exclaimed, "It's Poppleton! Let's make Cherry Su sick in bed and Poppleton helps her." Yesenia and Andrew nodded and the three children chatted about the chapter from *Poppleton* (Rylant) that they had just heard as a read-aloud.

The startling thing about this conversation was that it occurred among three children who were usually silent during whole-class discussions following read-aloud. The conversation Jocelyn, Andrew, and Yesenia had as they reenacted a story about Poppleton revealed language abilities that those youngsters had not shown during other portions of the school day—

and this allowed the teacher to raise her expectations across the entire day. As this example illustrates, it is not unusual for children to demonstrate proficiencies in choice time that can then be called upon when children talk about books and about their own writing, too. When teachers know their ELLs' levels of language proficiency, they can coach children to work within their zones of proximal development (Krashen and Terrell 1983). (See Figure 2.1.)

Choice time workshop is a powerful structure for ELLs for many reasons:

▶ It is safe.
▶ It is visual and hands-on.
▶ It occurs within a sea of language.
▶ It is accessible to everyone.
▶ It connects to other parts of the day.

Stage 1: Preproduction/ Silent	Stage 2: Early Production	Stage 3: Speech Emergence	Stage 4: Intermediate Fluency	Stage 5: Advanced Fluency
Students tend to understand more than they can say. Students often rely on gestures to communicate.	Students tend to listen with greater understanding and can produce some English words and short phrases.	Students usually speak in present tense and simple sentences. Tenses and simple pronouns are often confused.	Students often sound fluent with social language and they approximate academic language, but it can be hard for them to really follow stories told in past tense.	Students produce English with varied grammatical structures and vocabulary.

FIG. 2.1 *Levels of English Language Proficiency*

Choice Time Workshop Is Safe

To teach well, a teacher must put himself in the shoes of learners and empathize with their experience. How important it is, then, for a teacher to pause and think, "When have I been called upon to struggle at something, to be a beginner? When have I needed to be a public learner, working alongside others who were much more successful?" For most adults, it is not easy to recall times as public learners, and it is especially difficult to think of times one has struggled to learn and yet continued to persevere. It is important, then, to pause and realize that requesting that an ELL continue to use English as best he or she can is asking a lot of these children. The teacher must be sure to provide learners with the required conditions, and foremost among these is an environment in which it is OK to approximate, to make errors, to mess up. It is vastly easier to learn if the learner feels safe enough that he or she can take risks with language and learning. Stephen Krashen's theory of second language acquisition suggests that certain affective variables, such as low self-esteem, nervousness, and boredom, can create a filter, blocking the processing of incoming information. For successful language acquisition to occur, the filter must be low (Freeman and Freeman 2007). Choice time lowers the affective filter for ELLs—and for children who are also involved in reading and writing workshops, choice time workshops are especially comforting because of the familiarity of the workshop structure. For these children, the predictable nature of a workshop allows them to anticipate what will happen next, adding to their sense of security and allowing them to be brave risk takers with language.

Choice Time Workshop Is Visual and Hands-On

During choice time workshop, the language that children use and hear is apt to be comprehensible. Choice time workshops engage children in concrete, hands-on work. For example, during choice time, a child might assume the role of Poppleton, using gestures and pantomime to act out the story. This means that ELLs needn't rely on words alone to convey meaning. Art, blocks, and drama can all provide ELLs with the concrete supports they need to make and convey meaning.

Teachers also rely on the use of concrete, visual materials and on repetition and gestures to scaffold ELLs' work (Gibbons 1993). Minilessons become more comprehensible when teachers demonstrate using blocks, art, or drama. Often, in fact, a teacher will demonstrate using all of these modalities over successive days, allowing ELLs to hear and experience the content and vocabulary several times. For example, I (Cheryl) recently convened a group of children and said to them, "One thing we can do when we are done with our projects in choice time workshop is look at them again and add on to them to make them better." Then I showed children how I finished building a block tower and then, instead of knocking it down, looked at it again and added a triangle block to the top for a roof. On the next day, I taught almost the same lesson, using the same language, only this time I made my point by looking at my completed painting of my dog and thinking aloud, "How can I make this even better?" Then, using different-colored paints, I added some spots to the dog's fur and his collar. This kind of concrete demonstration sets children up to be successful as they go off and work in the stations, as it involves *showing* children what you want them to do, not just telling them.

Choice Time Workshop Occurs Within a Sea of Social Language

After the minilesson, children go off to work in one of the various stations and in each station, they represent their thinking through a different system (or modality). As children build, act, and draw, they also talk about what they are doing; the hands-on work provides them with a context for all their spoken language. For example, as Jason, an ELL in the speech emergence stage of language proficiency, and his friend Anthony worked to build a block car garage, they carried on this conversation:

ANTHONY: Jason, will you get the square short blocks for me?

JASON: This one? [*Points to triangle*]

ANTHONY: No, not that one.

JASON: [*Points to the right one and looks up, questioning*]

ANTHONY: Yeah, that one. OK, now the triangle.

JASON: [*Hands Anthony the triangle*]

ANTHONY: [*Referring to his structure*] This is nice, right?

JASON: Yeah. So this block is a car.

ANTHONY: Yeah.

During this brief interaction, Jason was learning English in context. He was given comprehensible input, and that input allowed him to learn abstract concepts, including the language of size and shapes. He was also simultaneously participating in the social language of listening, responding, and following directions. Partners such as Anthony play a role in making language comprehensible. When ELLs are paired with more proficient English speakers, everyone benefits. Important lessons happen when a child in the art station says to another child (while gesturing to her painting),"Look! I just made a heart!"

Choice Time Workshop Is Accessible to Everyone

It is incredibly important that during choice time workshops, teachers communicate that the class expectations pertain to everyone, including ELLs at all stages of language acquisition. For example, during cleanup time, teachers expect ELLs to pick up their work just like everyone else. If a language barrier prevents a child from understanding what is being asked, then the teacher needs to do everything in his power to make that language comprehensible so that expectations can truly pertain to everyone. For example, if a child needs to put the crayons away and does not understand this English command, the teacher can physically demonstrate what he wants the child to do. If the teacher wants to know the name of a block structure and if the teacher expects the child will communicate, the child will probably rise to the occasion. The important thing is that once a teacher has given an ELL child the wait time and the trust necessary so that the youngster does rise to the occasion, this one episode can raise expectations in dramatic ways. The teacher can extrapolate for the child, saying, "Do you see how you *did* talk, and it worked?" The teacher can also make sure that other children notice what the ELL can do so that children, as well as adults, begin to expect more of the learner. For example, one day during choice time workshop, I (Alison) pulled up alongside Nayeli, who was in the preproduction/silent stage of language acquisition. She was painting a picture in the art station. I asked her, "What are you making?"

Some of the kids in the class intervened to warn me off. "She doesn't speak English," one of them said, as though to say, "Don't talk to her; she can't talk."

My response to them was "Nayeli is learning English, and she understands a lot more than she can say. We need to help Nayeli understand what we are saying to her." Then I continued my conference with Nayeli. "So, Nayeli, what are you making?" I then nodded expectantly as if to say, "I believe that you understand what I am saying."

When she didn't answer, I followed up with some yes-or-no questions. "Is this you?" I asked as I pointed to the picture of the little girl. She nodded.

I pointed to her picture again and asked, "Is this a snake?" While I said *snake*, I made a snake movement with my body. She smiled and nodded again. Then I asked her, while acting it out, "So what happened? Did the snake bite you?" She then laughed and shook her head no. Then I asked, while acting out the motions, "Were you scared?" She smiled and nodded. So I pointed to her face in her picture and said, "So in your picture you can make your face look scared." I acted out scared again and had her do it with me, and then she changed the mouth in her painting to an *O* to show herself being scared.

I then said to the children who were painting with Nayeli, "See how Nayeli and I could have a conversation? When you talk with Nayeli, act out what you are saying like I did, and she will understand." This conference was important for many reasons. First, I was able to convey to Nayeli that I had high expectations of her, and she rose to the occasion, which allowed us to communicate. Second, these high expectations were modeled for the other children who were working near her, so that they too could have high expectations of her and of themselves as conversational partners for her. Third, I was able to model for Nayeli's classmates how to communicate with Nayeli so that she could receive more comprehensible input from her peers. The social environment in a classroom can make all the difference for a language learner. A teacher's job is not only to interact well with our ELLs but also to do everything in his power to be sure others do so as well.

Choice Time Workshop Connects to Other Parts of the Day

Often in choice time, children play with themes and characters that are rooted in the books they hear during read-aloud time and books they read during the reading workshop. Other times, choice time is linked to the studies that children are doing in science, social studies, or writing. For example, later in the year, there is a choice time unit of study that aims to invite children to function as a scientist. In the drama area during this time, two children might lie on their backs and pretend to watch clouds together, talking about the cumulus clouds, the thunderheads. Then, again, children might, during this choice time workshop, make a mural depicting clouds or pretend to be clouds of various kinds. (See Figure. 2.2.)

It is helpful to a learner if that child can bring the content or language from one area of curriculum to another area. For example, during the writing workshop, children might retell true stories from their lives, and they might use their fingers as a scaffold for doing this, with the child touching one finger and then the next as they proceed, in sequence, through the

Choice Time Workshop Units of Study	Writing Workshop Units of Study	Reading Workshop Units of Study
Unit 1: Planning and Pursuing Collaborative Projects	Launching a Writing Workshop (becoming independent with the habits, routines, and structures of writing workshop)	Readers Build Good Habits
Unit 2: Story Play	Personal Narrative	Readers Read Emergent Storybooks (K) Readers Think and Talk About Books to Grow Ideas (1) Character Study (2)
Unit 3 and 4: Planning and Inventing Projects Based in Social Studies or Science	All-About Books (nonfiction reports on personal topics of expertise)	Nonfiction Reading
Unit 5 and 6: Planning and Inventing Interest-Based Projects	Independent Writing Projects and Author Studies (another variation on independent writing projects)	Interest-Based Projects

FIG. 2.2 *One Possible Way to Align Choice Time and Reading and Writing Workshops for K–2 Learners*

step-by-step narrative. During the choice time workshop, after children work in their separate stations for forty minutes, the teacher might suggest that children meet with someone who had not shared their activity and that they tell each other about the work they just did. "Use your fingers," the teacher might say. "Touch each finger as you progress to the next portion of the story of your work." Similar cross-fertilization occurred recently when a few children in a bilingual kindergarten class at P.S. 112 in East Harlem made pineapple smoothies in a make-believe blender. Later, when it came time for those children to write procedural pieces in the writing workshop, the teacher was able to suggest they start this off by writing directions for the pineapple smoothies they'd just made together.

"How did you make them?" the teacher asked. "What did you do first?" When the children started telling the teacher what amounted to a how-to text, using the language of procedural texts, the teacher scribed this quickly for them and then read it back, saying to them, "You just told us a how-to book for *How to Make Smoothies*! Now you just need to write those directions." Children already had rehearsed the language and they had a concrete reference in mind to help them write. Throughout that writing unit, the teacher left how-to paper at the stations during choice time workshop, and she often asked children to write how-to texts immediately after they created something during choice time. In this way, the children began to see that writing how-to texts is a playful and purposeful activity.

David and Yvonne Freeman (2007) emphasize that ELLs benefit if teachers are able to align instruction across disciplines. For example, when a teacher uses similar teaching terminology in both choice time and the reading workshop, the concrete, embedded nature of choice time can help children grasp the meaning of particular bits of academic language, giving these children a leg up when those same terms are later used in the reading workshop. If a child acts out a mean troll in the dramatic play center, and the teacher muses, "What motivates him to be so mean, do you think? Why is he so mean?" and this leads to a whole discussion about that troll's reasons for being so mad, then if there is a discussion during the reading workshop about a character's motivation, children will approach that conversation differently. In Figure 2.2, notice that many teachers align units of study in choice time and reading workshop and writing workshop so that, for example, during October or November, children might be retelling and revising favorite stories through story play during choice time, writing true stories in the writing workshop, and reading and retelling stories during the reading workshop. (Of course, kindergartners cannot usually read print during the first month or two of the school year, but these children can approximate reading, storytelling their way through books that they know well.) The important thing to notice is that when reading, writing, and choice time are aligned, ELL children are able to explore vocabulary and concepts across the day, and this often means that abstract terms become more concrete.

CHAPTER THREE

Unit 1: Planning and Pursuing Collaborative Projects

In a choice time workshop, during the first four to six weeks of the year, we teach a unit of study that helps children work together to plan and pursue their own important projects during choice time. Whether students are working in the block, drama, or art station, they learn to decide upon and plan a shared project and to problem solve together. In a sense, this unit is about the process of creating a project—and it is not a coincidence that meanwhile, during the writing workshop, children are learning the process of creating stories. Children learn to use language to plan, negotiate decisions, instruct, clarify meaning, and critique—and meanwhile they learn to work with blocks, art materials, and their imaginations to pursue their own wonderful ideas.

Every unit of study unfolds as a story unfolds: with a beginning, middle, and end. Teachers waste no time before launching children into the choice time workshop, usually starting with minilessons that induct children into the structures, routines, and responsibilities of choice time. Teachers who lead workshops across their curriculum will need to teach students to convene in a meeting area, moving quickly to their assigned rug spots, and to teach them that sometimes during a minilesson they will need to turn and work with a partner. The transitions between watching and listening to a teacher, then turning to talk for a minute or two with a partner, then returning their attention to the teacher need to become smooth, and the choice time workshop is a good place to teach these classroom routines because frankly, children are especially interested in what the teacher has to say when that instruction involves concrete materials such as paints, clay, blocks and when it involves very clear strategies such as the step-by-step procedures involved in learning to use the stapler. That is, teachers can use choice time as a forum for inducting children into the norms and behaviors of workshop teaching, and then teachers can transfer what children learn during the choice time workshop into the reading and writing workshop as well.

During the first unit, children not only learn how to function in a choice time workshop, they also learn the processes for going about working on a project with a cluster of colleagues. Sometimes children are apt to start work simply by reaching for some materials and tools. They take hold of a marker or reach for clay, and then let ideas and plans emerge from the material. This might work for any one individual, but it is less apt to work for a group of children who are hoping to collaborate on a shared endeavor. When working together in a choice time station, then, it usually works better if children first think and talk about their ideas, selecting one, and only then use materials to fashion that idea. In choice time, then, as in reading and writing, they learn to think and talk—to rehearse—before plunging into a project. Before plunging into a project, children also need to access the appropriate tools. Then, too, they benefit from learning that when working toward a goal, it is not uncommon to run into problems. Frequently, there will be trouble. When a person encounters trouble, this can be a time to simply throw in the towel and quit—or, ideally, it can be a time to think and talk about what might not be working and to try another approach—and that's usually the better response. Then, too, once children have worked for a time on a project, they need to pull back and think, "How could I do this even better?" and "What else can I add?"

Of course, when this planning and assessing and revising is done collaboratively, this demands a terrific amount of language. Children not only need to use words, they need to use words to support higher-level thinking. And they need to not only talk but also to listen to each other. They need to learn to listen to and consider the ideas and perspectives of a partner, talking through those ideas and negotiating decisions.

Unit Goals

A Sense of Agency

Learning is not something that one person can do for another. Instead, the learner must be the person who does the learning. How important it is, then, that children bring a sense of personal agency to school and operate with independence and initiative. This is a particularly important goal for ELLs, especially in the bustling activity of an early childhood classroom, where it is often more expedient for a teacher to do something *for* such children rather than have them do it on their own. ELLs may *appear* to be passive, although they are actively listening—their behavior may be misinterpreted as a sign of helplessness or lack of comprehension. The choice time workshop provides large chunks of time for children to devise and pursue plans, accessing the materials they need, planning their procedure, working in pairs and triads as the teacher circulates. The work is multilevel enough that everyone can work intensely, proactively.

Collaboration

Choice time workshop provides opportunities for children at all stages of language development to share their thinking and ideas in a collaborative community. Because all the children in one station are expected to jointly contribute to a shared experience, they need to use language to suggest and consider options, to name and resolve problems, to dole out roles as well as to learn from each other. Children share materials as a common space in a station, and more importantly, they share ideas.

Getting Started in Unit 1

There are lots of possible ways to launch a choice time workshop. Some teachers induct children into this part of the school day by helping children understand how this workop will go. "Thinkers," a teacher might say, "This year, we will have a special time of the day when you'll use your own ideas to do some amazing work." The teacher might then take children on a tour of the different stations in the classroom, helping them imagine possibilities for how their work could go in each station. As the teacher brings children into the block station, she shows the children the system for storing different blocks in different places, using pictures of the block shapes to organize this storage system. The teacher might then bring the children into the art station. "This is the art station. In this station you will be an artist. You might choose to paint pictures on the easel or to draw and color at the art table." The teacher can show children how to put on smock and to use the easel, reminding them to avoid mixing the brushes with different colors. The teacher might also show the future artists what to do with their work when they're finished. In a similar fashion, the teacher continues touring the stations, showing children the work they could do in the listening station, the puzzle station, and so forth. Then, convening the children, the teacher can say, "Tomorrow you will get to choose the station in which you'd like to work. Your homework is to start thinking of a few choices in your mind and think also about what you might want to create in your station!"

By the second or third day of the choice time workshop, the teacher will probably need to introduce the choice board or whatever other structure is used for channeling children into the different stations. When the children are gathered on the carpet, the teacher might say, "Thinkers, yesterday we saw all of the different stations in the classroom and began to imagine some of the work we can do in each of those stations.

And last night you thought about the stations you'd like to explore first. For us to do our best work in choice time workshop, only a certain number of children can work in each station." An explanation might be provided: "It's sort of the same as swimming. Last week, the pool was so crowded that I couldn't really swim. So the next day, I went swimming really early in the morning when not too many people were there, so I was able to do some really good swimming. It's not only swimmers who need space. All of us, as workers, need space to create." The teacher could then show the children a choice board, which has a picture of each station with places for children to put their names (see Figure 3.1). Many teachers choose the number of children that each station can contain, basing this on the amount of space and materials in that station.

FIG. 3.1 *Choice Board*

"So, thinkers, this means that before choice time, you will want to think of a couple choices in your mind in case you don't get your first choice." Teachers can decide which children get first dibs. Some teachers will proceed through the class list in alphabetical order, moving down the list each day. Other teachers organize the process by suggesting that on Mondays the first row of children in the meeting area gets first choice; on Tuesdays, the second row gets first choice; and so on. When children choose a station, often they will put their name underneath the station title on the choice board.

Some children will get upset when they don't get their first choice, but when they understand the system they learn to make backup choices. This disappointment on that first day can be a powerful lead-in to a class discussion on the importance of taking turns. Some children will actually offer their spots to disappointed classmates.

As children go off to work, the teacher can quickly move from station to station, offering compliments and tips to students as they work. Inevitably a child will ask on this first day, "Can I go to another station?" This is an important opportunity for a mid-workshop teaching moment. In reading and writing workshop, when a child finishes writing a text or reading a book, that child doesn't say, "I'm done" and move on to another subject but instead, that child simply starts the next reading or writing project. Similarly, teachers can instruct students that in choice time workshop, the child must stay in one station for the entire work time. Teachers can reiterate this important expectation when they call children back to the carpet at the end of work time. "Thinkers, I saw Nayeli doing something very smart today. When she was finished painting her picture in the art station, instead of trying to leave and go to another station, she realized that in choice time workshop, we stay in our station the *whole* time. So, after she finished painting one picture, she thought about what else she could do in her station. She realized that she could add on to her picture to make it better or she could make another picture. You can all do the same thing in your stations. So starting to-morrow and from now on, when you are finished making something in your station, you can either make that project better or you can make something else, but stay in your sta-tion the *whole* time. Let's write that up on a chart so that we don't forget!" The teacher might want to create a chart with students titled "What to Do When You Are Done with Your Work in Your Station." Children soon internalize the impor-tance of persevering, especially because they are learning stamina while working in the reading and writing workshop as well as during choice time.

Language Functions Supported in This Unit

Children learn language when they have many different reasons to use language and therefore are channeled to work within lots of different genre (Chen and Mora-Flores 2006). In this unit, many of the language functions explicitly taught include:

- agreeing and disagreeing
- getting along with peers
- planning a project with a partner
- working on a project with a friend

- playing a game with a friend
- asking for assistance
- sharing an exciting event
- describing how one is feeling
- apologizing
- asking for permission
- commanding/giving instructions
- following directions
- denying/refusing
- expressing likes and dislikes
- evaluating
- predicting
- suggesting
- wishing and hoping

Language functions are embedded in all the work that children do during the choice time workshop, and in all the teaching. When students learn to put away their materials, for example, teachers use conditional language saying *"If you do this, then. . . ."* Meaning is carried by the presence of artifacts—the materials to be put away—and by body movements and gestures. This provides scaffold for ELLs to understand language.

How It Looks in the Stations

Blocks

In the block areas, teachers teach children to work collaboratively on one large project, to talk about and agree upon a shared plan before starting, to revise the block creation once it is made, to use the block creation as a site for reenactments (perhaps using plastic action figures). The teacher can suggest children use language to present several possibilities, using phrases such as "or could we . . ." and "another ideas is. . . ." Teachers can teach children to take turns, to listen to each other's ideas and talk back to those ideas, to agree and disagree to provide reasons. It's a stretch, then, to call the block station a block station—it is actually a language station!

Although initially this station contains only the blocks themselves, later it helps to add accessories such as cars, paper, and pencils, and action figures. These can be powerful ways to extend and teach vocabulary for ELLs and to increase their levels of engagement.

Drama

As in the block station, the drama station should have open-ended materials: fabric for children to create costumes, hollow blocks for building settings and furniture, and butcher block paper and art materials for creating needed props. As the unit continues, add accessories gradually and provide opportunities to teach vocabulary by showing children real objects (see Figure 3.2). As in the block station, teachers can add photos or images to shelves as a scaffold for directing children to put materials back in the appropriate places.

Art

Materials in the art station could include various types of paper, crayons, markers, colored pencils, glue, scissors, paint,

FIG. 3.2 *Joshua and Anthony Dramatizing Their Recent Visit to a Pizza Shop*

brushes, and clay or play dough, and perhaps a chart with photos of kids using the materials in different ways: painting, sculpting with clay or play dough, working on collage, and using colored pencils, crayons, and markers. Such a chart not only suggests activities, it also helps children become accustomed to using a chart as a source of ideas for productive activities. It's fun to have a box of cool stuff that has been collected and can be used in various projects; it's always interesting to see what kids do with these materials (see Figure 3.3).

FIG. 3.3 *Brianna Contributing to a Mural in the Art Station*

Minilessons with Scaffolds for English Language Learners

A teacher will want to use every imaginable method to be sure that minilessons are comprehensible to all children. There are many ways in which the architecture of minilessons already supports ELLs. Because every workshop begins with a five- or ten-minute minilessons, children are cued to expect that when the teacher convenes the class on the carpet, she will try to teach the children something that pertains to every station. When the teacher begins, she'll retell lessons the children already learned and point to those teaching points on a chart. Then she'll signal the new content by using words such as, "Today I want to teach you . . ." before naming the day's teaching point. It will be repeated four or five times within the brief lesson and recorded on chart paper. The teacher will demonstrate what she wants children to do. When she talks about steps, she uses her fingers to gesture step one, step two. She uses artifacts. Children do a lot of work with partners. ELLs benefit by being paired with children who are ahead of them in language development and who can serve as language models. Beginning speakers benefit from being paired with someone who speaks their native language as well as English, if possible. In these and other ways, minilessons can have scaffolds for ELLs.

For children in the beginning stages of language acquisition, it is helpful if the teacher can preview the content of the minilesson in the child's first language. A teacher might rely on another child for this, one who speaks the same native language as the ELL. For example, in a minilesson about creating the setting for our writing, right before the minilesson, the teacher could ask Anthony, who speaks English and Spanish, to tell his partner, Jason (a beginning speaker) what the minilesson will be about. "Anthony, our minilesson today is about creating a setting for the stories we are writing. You know how Corduroy [the teacher pointed to a page in the book that showed Lisa and her mom in the toy store] takes place in a department store? That is the setting. Please tell Jason in Spanish what our lesson is about."

Most of the lessons for this unit support students in planning what they will work on and how they will go about that work. Students will also need support for their collaboration.

Supporting Planning in Choice Time Workshop

One major goal of this first unit of study is to teach students how to be planful as part of the workshop routine. In writing workshop, teachers help students become more planful, teaching them to think of their story first and only then to draw a picture to represent that story. The same strategy applies in choice time workshop. As mentioned before, many students simply pick up the materials and then let the materials dictate what they will do, instead of first generating a meaning, a content, and a plan. During choice time, we teach children that it usually works best to plan, and to do this with their colleagues. The plan, then, can channel children's choice of materials. For example, when Druzela and Samuel arrived in the dramatic play station, they immediately started sorting through a box of fabrics and began wrapping the various swatches around themselves. Samuel stopped her, saying, "We is playing McDonald's. Let's make what those french fry ladies wear." With this sense of direction, the two partners found some red and yellow fabric and make a spectacular "french fry lady" outfit. Figure 3.4 is an example of a minilesson that helps children plan and make planning part of their routine for choice time workshop.

Connection and Teaching Point

"Thinkers, yesterday Sophie sorted through all our blocks, looking for something. 'I'm making a house so I need the long blocks,' she said. It was smart of her to first decide what she was making and then decide the materials she needed for that project."

"Thinkers, today I want to teach you that before we start playing, we can take a second to think, 'What do I want to do?' We can think about all the stuff we could perhaps do and then choose the best idea."

The teacher reveals a chart titled, "Some Ways to Plan for Our Work in Choice Time Workshop." Under the title is the teaching point already written out. Next to the teaching point is a picture of a child in the block station with a speech bubble coming out of his mouth saying, "What do I want to do?"

Demonstration

"Watch me as I work in the art station and notice what I do first."

The teacher begins by plunging directly into work with the materials, bypassing the planning she'd just learned to do. "Oh look! Here are foamy shapes and glue. I'll stick these on some paper!"

Then the teacher self-corrects. "Oh wait . . . I said that I would try to think of what I want to do first before I just start playing. OK, let me think, 'What do I want to do?' Hmm, let me see. . . ."

At this point she begins to look around at the different materials. She looks at the art easel, which has a blank sheet of paper hanging on it, and at the different trays of paper and markers laid out on the supply shelves.

"I could paint a picture of a rainbow, or I could make a picture of me and my mom, or I could make a card for my dad." (Notice that I come up with a couple of possible ideas.)

FIG. 3.4 *Transcript of a Minilesson on Planning*

"Let me think about which idea I want to do first. I think I'll start by making a card for my dad because it is his birthday tomorrow and I really want to make him something."

"Thinkers, did you see that I didn't just pick up the first thing I saw and start playing with it? Instead I paused for a second and looked around and thought about the things I could do and asked myself, 'What do I want to do?' I came up with several possibilities and then I picked the best idea. You can do the same thing in your stations."

Active Engagement

"Thinkers, I want you to close your eyes and picture the station you'll be in to today and think, 'What do I want to do?' Then, once you have some ideas, turn and tell your partner what you are thinking and which idea you might choose. You can look up at the choice board to help you."

The choice board has photographs of all the different stations. This visual scaffold can be a quick reminder of what is in the stations, but it also can be a way for ELLs at the beginning stages of language proficiency to communicate with their partners, as they can point to different items in the pictures.

After listening to a few partnerships, the teacher calls the students back together. "Wow, I heard so many great ideas! I heard Jessica saying that she is going to drama today," the teacher says, pointing to the picture of the drama station on the choice board, "and she might pretend either that she's working in a pizza shop or that she's a princess. Then I heard Jacqueline say she is going to blocks and she is going to build either a house or our school!"

Link to Ongoing Work

"So, thinkers, from now on, before you start playing in your stations, you can take a second to think, 'What do I want to do?' and then decide what you will do in our station based on that."

FIG. 3.4 *Continued*

Other Possibilities for Minilessons to Support Planning

▶ Planning by picturing the finished project
We can plan how our projects will go by picturing our idea in our mind, and saying to ourselves, "What do I see?" Then we can try and create our mind picture in our stations.

▶ Planning by naming what we'll do when we're finished
When station partners are finished creating their projects together, one thing we can plan to do is talk about our favorite parts of the project and why it is our favorite part. We can say, "My favorite part is...." Sometimes this gives us the idea to add to our favorite parts.

▶ Planning by picturing it in the real world
Once we decide to make something—whether we're making it with blocks, with paint, with clay, or with our own movements, we usually think, "What is this thing that I am making really like in the real world? How can I make a block structure, a drawing, a drama, that captures the truth of this thing?" This means that first, we think about—we envision—whatever it is we will represent, then we take what's in our mind, and we try to capture it on the paper or in the block structure. If we are making a barn out of blocks, we need to start by envisioning a barn. Afterward, we pull back and look at what we've made, and we think, "What did I leave out? What else can I add?"

▶ Planning to start with the big picture and add details
When we're making something—a horse barn, a garage, a castle surrounded by walls—we usually first make the broad outlines of that thing. After we make the big outline of our

subject, we usually go back and think, 'What details can I add?" If we've made a horse barn, after we build the broad outline of the barn, we step back and look over what we've made. We think, "OK, I have a stall for each horse. But where will the hay be kept? The saddles?" That is, we think about the details, and add the fine points onto what we have made.

▶ Planning to overcome trouble
Very often, when we are making something, we run into trouble. The roof caves in. The dog we've painted looks more like a horse. When you run into trouble, you could just say, "Oh forget it." But it is far better to respond to trouble by thinking, "What solutions might there be that I haven't yet considered?" and to try your work again, differently.

▶ Planning to make the project even better instead of finishing the first time
When we think we are finished with a project, instead of saying, "I'm done," we can ask ourselves, "What can I do to make my project better?" or "What else can I create in this station?" And then we keep working until choice time workshop is over.

▶ Planning by looking at the materials in the station and thinking, "What could I make?"
A teacher could start with open-ended materials in all the stations (see "How It Looks in the Stations" on page 32). Later, she can add accessories that can be used for teaching vocabulary, such as different kinds of vehicles, people, and animals, fabric of various textures for creating costumes, and specific props to support the work the

children are doing (playing restaurant, shoe store, and so on).

- Planning by looking through favorite read-alouds and thinking, "What could I make?"

  If familiar read-alouds are stored near stations, children can draw on these as they work. If *Mike Mulligan and His Steam Shovel* (Burton 1939) is near the block area, chances are good children might recreate the building project that is at the heart of that story. Books can provide a useful visual scaffold for ELLs. It is important to model how to use these books before placing them in the stations. Again, children are thinking in terms of planning and predicting possible outcomes. The books provide visual aids that will give ELLs an important context for language.

Conferences

As children work—whether they are working as artists, builders, writers, or readers—teachers move among them, crouching low, pulling close, to understand what it is that children are trying to do. If a child stops what he or she is doing as the teacher draws close, the teacher gestures, "Keep going. Don't mind me." Then she listens and observes, thinking, as she does this, "What is this youngster trying to do?" Sometimes the teacher comes right out and asks the child to tell what he is aiming to accomplish and how he feels about the work. "Can you explain what you are working on?" the teacher might ask. "What are you trying to do? How's it going?" Then the teacher watches and listens to what the child says and does. The teacher might think, "What is the child almost but not quite able to do? How can I intervene in ways that help not only with today's work but also in ways that will transfer to other days?" These interactions—called conferences—are at the heart of any workshop. There are three main ways that a conference can proceed: 1) The teacher can interject lean prompts into the child's ongoing work, almost providing language overlays; 2) the teacher can interview and observe for a bit, and then stop the child's ongoing work to deliver what is essentially a private minilesson, complete with an explicit teaching point, usually prefaced by a comment such as, "Can I teach you one thing?"; and 3) teachers can confer to support one child or to support a partnership or small group of children working together.

Coaching Conferences

Coaching conferences for ELLs often include language coaching. Jose says to Emma. "Make . . ." and then instead of telling her to draw a door, he uses his finger to sketch the shape he hopes she will draw onto their picture of a house. The teacher, listening in, says quietly, "Use words," and points to her mouth. She repeats Jose's first word, *make*, and then lets him know she'd like him to try to tell Emily what it is that he wants her to draw. Jose answers in Spanish, and she nods, and says the word in English. Jose nods and is all set to make his next point to Emma, but the teacher says, "Repeat it" and then, when Jose doesn't seem to grasp her content, she might provide a language model. "Emma, make a door," and then gesture for Jose to repeat it. This teacher is coaching. She is interjecting lean prompts into Jose's ongoing work, adjusting the amount of support she provides as she takes her cues from Jose.

If Jose had been in the preproduction/silent stage of language acquisition, the teacher might have instead asked him questions that could be answered with just a yes or a no. She might have said, "Jose, do you want Emma to draw a door? A door [and she could gesture to show a door] or a window?"

Children in the intermediate stage benefit from language prompts that scaffold their partner talk. A language prompt chart would help to scaffold their talk. The chart could contain phrases such as, "Maybe we could make. . . ."

Language coaching conferences look different with children at different stages of language acquisition. When conferring with a child in the preproduction/silent stage, it helps to ask yes-or-no questions and use visuals, tone, and gestures to communicate. For example, when pulling up alongside a child in the block station, a teacher could begin by asking, "What are you making?" If the child doesn't answer, the teacher could follow up with a yes-or-no question such as, "Is this a house?" When the child nods or says yes, the teacher can respond with "Oh, so you are building a house!" thereby providing a language model. In conferences, assessment happens on the run, and teaching is adaptive.

Research/Decide/Teach Conferences

The teacher pulls close to observe as two children, sitting alongside each other, build separate block houses. The children each keep a store of blocks between their legs, drawing from this repository, but each child runs into limitations because the block supply is not extensive. One child tries to raid the other's storehouse and a brief tussle ensues. Watching this for a minute, the teacher says, "I see you are each making a little house. But Marco, I see that you want to make a roof for house [the teacher gestures to where the roof will go] but, oh no! No more blocks! [Raising her hands in despair, the teacher acts out the impasse.] How about if you put your two houses together and make one big one! [Again, the teacher gestures showing that the two houses could be slid into one bigger house.] It could have two floors and a roof! Will you try that?"

The children look a bit hesitant, but the teacher brings out paper and a pen. "It could be a castle! How should it look?" and she turns the paper over to Marco. The two boys begin working together on a shared plan. After watching for a minute, the teacher says, "In blocks, the two of you [she points to show one person, and the next] need to make one thing. First [she gestures to show number one] you draw [and she points to the picture]. Then [she gestures to show the number two] you build with the blocks."

Partnership Conferences

In all workshops, children spend time working with partners or small groups. These relationships are especially important in classrooms that brim with ELLs. In a partnership conference, the teacher coaches students to work well together. When one child is an ELL, the teacher will often coach the more proficient English speaker to use the same strategies that teachers use to support a child's language comprehension. For example, the teacher can teach the more proficient child to use gestures to communicate, to ask yes-or-no questions, to provide wait time, and to restate the language learner's less complete phrases as complete sentences. The teacher can also coach the more proficient speaker to ask his or her partner questions. For example, the teacher could coach a child to ask his station partner a question, such as "What are you making?" The teacher can do this by whispering into the child's ear, "Say, 'What are you making?'" Then when the partner answers, the teacher can coach her to ask return the question, asking, "What are *you* making?" The goal is to help the children carry on a conversation with each other. (See Figure 3.5.)

Teaching Shares

At the end of choice time workshop each day, children reconvene on the carpet for the teaching share. This is an opportunity to work on language development. Because children are all working in different stations, it is important for them to share so they can hear some of the work that peers in other stations have done. This often gives kids ideas for work that they could be doing. The teacher can structure the share in different ways. One way is to have a headline share, where one representative from each station tells the class what the group worked on in that station. Before sharing with the class, the station partners get together and discuss what headline the representative will share. This is an important structure for ELLs because they have the opportunity to hear

FIG. 3.5 *Teacher, Cara Biggane, Conducting a Partnership Conference*

language and rehearse it aloud in a small-group setting before sharing it aloud with the whole group. Depending on their level of language proficiency, some children may rehearse in their native language before reporting back to the large group in English.

A teacher can also use the teaching share as a time to problem solve predictable trouble or share station-specific tips, such as how to build a sturdy block structure or how to use scissors to create a fringe effect on an art picture.

Publication

In the writing workshop, units of study end with a celebration. Prior to this, children look over their work and select their best work, then fix this up and fancy it up in preparation for publication and celebration. Teachers who lead choice time workshops find that in a similar manner, it helps to end a unit with a celebration.

Children will be eager for an opportunity to go public with their projects. Before the celebration, the teacher should encourage students to think about choosing a single project—a single block structure, art project, or dramatic performance—to share. Ideally, the celebration should spotlight not only the projects children have created but also the skills children have developed during the unit. For example, the teacher might have children share not only the airport that they built in the block station but also the sketches that they used to plan that airport.

CHAPTER FOUR

Unit 2: Story Play

In the second choice time workshop unit, children are taught the skills and strategies they will need to reenact and to represent the stories they've been reading and writing. This unit begins with the teacher reading aloud a few memorable stories often enough that children come to know those stories, quite literally, by heart. Then children will tell and retell, act and reenact, those stories through the modalities of paint, clay, blocks, and drama. As children do this work, teachers teach minilessons that show students ways to more effectively retell and reenact familiar stories.

Within the unit, teachers teach children to retell stories by recreating the sequence of events, the plotline of the story. As part of this, teachers help children grasp what it means to tell something sequentially. The teacher might say, "What happened just before the billy goats tossed the troll over the bridge? Did this happen in the beginning of the story, or did other events happen first?" These sorts of questions often dominate the standardized tests that children encounter once

49

they are eight or nine years old, and oftentimes these tests are the first time that some children encounter phrases such as "What happened first? What was right before that?" It is important, then, that this unit helps children understand the academic language and concepts related to sequence and to the passage of time.

Whether children are writing stories, recalling stories they've read, or creating their own stories through story play, the stories they create tend at first to be underdeveloped, lacking elaboration and detail. These stories may contain a sequential plot, but not a lot more than that. "He did one thing, then the next, then the next." Once children have begun recreating and retelling stories through blocks, drama and art, teachers will want to lift the level of those stories, and the easiest way to do so is by encouraging children to make their stories more detailed from the start. The best way to bring out the detail in a story is to help the creator (or re-creator) of the story actually relive the drama, to see the place in her mind's eye, to reenact or envision the character doing one small activity, with great detail, then the next, then the next. To re-enact The *Three Little Pigs*, the child playing the wolf will probably call out, "Let me in, let me in," and when the child playing the role of a pig answers, "Not by the hair of my chinny chin chin," the wolf probably, at first, blows at and pounces at the house, knocking it down. In a conference, the teacher can help the child playing the wolf character rethink what she probably did when the little pig announced he wouldn't let the wolf in. Did the wolf circle the house, thinking? Did he back up and take a gigantic breath of air and only then blow and blow on the house? Did he need to do that several times before the house blew over? The conferring and minilessons in this section of the unit of study will all be geared toward helping children actually assume the role of a character and enliven that character's part.

In the next part of the unit, teachers continue the work of helping children create and re-create stories that are more elaborate, but this time the teachers do so by helping children think about the elements of story. Teachers coach the child to consider the world in which the story is set, to flesh out each character so that that character takes on particular traits, and to think about whether, in this story, the main character wants something, runs into trouble, and finds a way to resolve those troubles. All of this, of course, happens while children relive stories that their teacher has read aloud to them many times. (It also happens during writing workshop and when children reenact their own true stories from their lives in order to write them).

The last section of the unit gives children time to prepare for a final celebration by choosing one story that they especially love and to recreate that one story using several different stations, different modalities. One cluster of children, then, might make a play about the "Three Little Pigs" and then recreate this story in both blocks and in art.

Unit Goals

Higher-Level Comprehension

In the beginning stages of language acquisition, ELLs often have ideas that they are not able to express through words.

This unit provides students with opportunities to represent their thinking through blocks, drama, and art. It is through these contextual experiences that students engage in higher-level comprehension skills such as, retelling, envisionment, inference, and interpretation.

Revision

Many children believe that when they complete a project that they are "done." In this unit, a goal is to develop the important habit of mind that good work is in a constant state of revision. Children are encouraged to revise their thinking about books they have heard read aloud, books they have read independently, and their own writing.

Getting Started in Unit 2

Using Read-Alouds to Inspire Story Play

Elizabeth Sulzby, a professor of education at the University of Michigan, researched children's literacy development, showing that when children have been read aloud to often and have grown up in literacy-rich environments, this helps them learn to read. Sulzby's research demonstrates that it is powerful indeed if a teacher selects a few stories, reads those books repeatedly, and then invites children to pretend to read those stories themselves. Over time, children's approximations of readings will become closer and closer to conventional reading. This research underlies this second unit of study. The essence of the unit is this: children hear stories read aloud repeatedly, then they represent and reenact and storytell those stories themselves.

In one kindergarten classroom, Samuel is carefully painting a retelling of *The Carrot Seed* (Krauss 1945), a book that Samuel's teacher has read aloud almost twenty times. The carrot in Samuel's painting is almost as big as he is. As Samuel paints, he says in a soft, gentle voice, "His mother said, 'I'm afraid it won't come up.'" Samuel's voice changes into a slightly taunting cadence as he says, "His big mean brother said, 'It won't come up.'" He continues, "All the people said, 'It won't come up.' But the little boy kept taking out the weeds and sprinkling the ground with water." Looking up, Samuel points out, "See, I can read the pages without even opening it up."

Sulzby's work is based on the premise that it is important to surround kids with richly textured storybooks, to read those books aloud multiple times, and then to invite children to read the book as well, relying on pictures and their memories of the text if they cannot yet read the actual words. As Sulzby says, "Learning to read and to write involves a re-conceptualization by the child of his/her language which had its beginning in oral contexts and functions. In other words, the acquisition of literacy can be said to involve a transition from oral language to written language" (1985, 460).

Marie Clay, a leader in the teaching of reading, once said, "Attention to the formal properties of print and correspondence with sound segments is the final step in a progression, not the entry point to understanding what written language is" (1991, 33). Clay said that when children hear repeated readings of storybooks and approximate those readings on their own, they develop "an awareness of plot and character, of meanings, and of language and words" (184).

Selecting Books for Read-Alouds

Sulzby outlines important criteria for selecting storybooks that will be memorable for children, books children will want to retell and reenact. She suggests that it is important for teachers to read aloud books that have been carefully chosen to fit these criteria:

- ❭ The book should have a strong, compelling story with a vivid plot and characters.

- ❭ The book should have a strong emotional appeal to children.

- ❭ The pictures in the book should clearly tell the story. The illustrations should be interesting and attractive because children will be using the pictures to make meaning of the story.

- ❭ The story should have complex language and should use literary language.

- ❭ Children should really love the book (because they will be hearing it over and over).

In addition, a book will be more appealing if it contains dialogue or repeated lines.

Here are some texts that fit these criteria and have been found effective and engaging:

Caps for Sale, by Esphyr Slobodkina (1987)
The Three Billy Goats Gruff, by Paul Galdone (1981)
Big Al, by Andrew Clemens (1997)
Peter's Chair, by Ezra Jack Keats (1998)
The Snowy Day, by Ezra Jack Keats (1976)
Harry the Dirty Dog, by Gene Zion (1976)
Corduroy, by Don Freeman (1968)
Leo the Late Bloomer, by Robert Kraus (1994)
The Carrot Seed, by Ruth Krauss (1945)
Are You My Mother? by P. D. Eastman (1960)
The Gingerbread Boy, by Paul Galdone (1975)
The Three Little Pigs, by Steven Kellogg (2002)
Jamaica's Find, by Juanita Havill (1987)

Using Just-Right Books to Inspire Story Play

In the choice time centers, children can reenact and storytell not only the books their teacher has read aloud, but also books that the children, themselves, have read. It will be important for children to bring the leveled books that they are reading during the reading workshop into their choice time stations. Maricella and Nikyah, first-grade reading partners, took the Level D text *Water Balloons* (Martin 2002) to the drama station and, after rereading the book several times, acted out Piggy and his dad playing hide-and-seek and throwing water balloons at each other. They decided that the next day they would select the art station so that they could create props to make their story more realistic.

Using Personal Narratives from Writing Workshop to Inspire Story Play

Children can also bring the stories that they and their class-mates have written into the choice time stations. In some classrooms, teachers place baskets of kids' published pieces in the stations to invite children to select a piece that they want to bring to life. If a child selects a story that he wrote earlier in the year and then reenacts that story, chances are good that the child will remember new details in ways that flesh out the original text and the child will want to revise that draft, adding to it. After creating a drama around Samuel's three-page book about hurting his leg when he went to the park with his Ti-Ti (aunt), he went back to the written text and added two pages to it. He added the dialogue that he and Wandalize (who played the role of his Ti-Ti) exchanged. Fati-mata returned to her piece about eating at McDonald's with her uncle and cousins after she painted detailed watercolor of the french fries, and this time she added three lines de-scribing the delectable food.

Language Functions Supported in This Unit

The first unit, described in Chapter 3, especially encouraged children to develop social language. This unit, on the other hand, encourages them to develop academic language including the following areas:

- ❯ retelling a story
- ❯ describing how a character in a book is feeling
- ❯ inferring what else a character might do
- ❯ predicting what might occur in a story
- ❯ creating a play or dramatizing a story

How It Looks in the Stations

Blocks

Children may take books they love into the block station (see Figure 4.1). For example, in Cara Biggane's first-grade class in the South Bronx, Nyah, Katherine, and Andrew created an adaptation of Paul Galdone's *The Gingerbread Boy* (1975) in the block station. Katherine suggested that the group change the setting from a small town to New York City. Their adaptation began as the children constructed a block bakery like the one they'd visited during a class trip to Rockefeller Center. To make this structure, the children found books that contained photos of Rockefeller Center and then used those photographs to help them create the setting for their bakery.

Drama

Give a six-year-old a plastic action figure and the child will begin to dramatize. Give the child a hat or a cloak or a weapon

FIG. 4.1 *Emory Retelling* The Three Billy Goats Gruff *in the Block Station*

(there's no denying it) and they step into roles. Drama is an essential part of childhood, and it is essential to reading and writing, too, for it is what a reader does when she gets "lost a story"—she dramatizes. Readers step into the shoes of a character. And writers envision in such a way that they write with vividness and power—they dramatize and capture that drama on the page so that the readers, too, can use language to experience vicariously. As kids retell, envision, interpret, synthesize, and adapt the stories they know and love through drama, they use written words to construct meanings, and do so by drawing on their own thoughts, knowledge, and experiences as well as on a close reading of texts.

It's best if classrooms can contain props for drama: hollow blocks for building sets, fabric for designing costumes, butcher block paper, wooden stools, or large cardboard boxes all help children create scenarios and step into roles. But the truth is that children need none of this. They simply need imagination, language, each other, time—and the teacher's encouragement.

Art

Children can create their own interpretations of stories using various art media. Samuel used mixed paints to create all shades of green when painting the meadow from *The Three Billy Goats Gruff* (Galdone 1981). He proudly proclaimed that he was painting the setting.

In the inquiry room at P.S. 277, kids created murals of *The Gingerbread Boy* (Ziefert 1995) and *Caps for Sale* (Slobodkina 1987) on butcher block paper using paint, markers, and collage materials. Children can also use the art station in this unit of study to create puppets of characters (from books they have read and stories they have written) and then use these puppets as props in the drama and block stations.

Minilessons with Scaffolds for English Language Learners

In the previous unit, children were taught expectations for choice time workshop and were given strategies to think, talk, problem solve, and collaborate. In this unit, children continue to do this work, but this time, they build and collaborate with blocks and paints to re-create stories—those they've heard, read, and written. This unit, then, supports not only social but also academic language development and it supports higher-level comprehension skills. The lessons in this unit fall into four broad categories:

- ▶ retelling favorite stories in stations
- ▶ retelling with detail
- ▶ retelling with a focus on story elements
- ▶ retelling in multiple modalities

Following are some *suggested* teaching points for mini-lessons in this unit, including scaffolds for ELLs. It is important to remember the needs of the kids when planning minilessons and to plan minilessons based on assessment.

Retelling Favorite Stories in Stations

Most moviegoers rehash favorite movies with their friends. "How 'bout the part when . . " they say. And, "Wasn't it amazing how. . . . " "Could you believe the way we. . . . " Readers respond similarly to books they love, phoning friends and family to say, "I gotta tell you about this book I just read. It starts out with. . . . " And in fact, the tendency to retell, to relive, to reminisce, is deeply ingrained in human beings. People attend a wedding, go on a vacation, live through a crisis . . . and their response is to retell and reexperience all that they've lived through. In this unit of study, teachers encourage children to retell through the medium of improvisational drama, art, blocks, and puppets. This is important work for lots of reasons—after all, retelling a book is often used as a prime indicator as to whether a child comprehended that book. When children retell stories they're heard, read, and written through art, drama, and blocks, they are engaged in work that is very close to the heart of what it means to read and to write.

Hearing repeated readings of a story is an important scaffold for ELLs. The carefully selected emergent storybook read-alouds provide clear pictures that support the story and the retelling. (See Figure 4.2.)

When a child hears or reads a story and then turns around to retell that story, it is very common for the child to first talk about what he just heard, just read—the story's end. Not surprisingly, this often leads to convoluted sequencing. This minilesson teaches children that to retell a story so others can follow it, it helps to start at the beginning and to proceed step-by-step in sequence, skipping over unimportant parts and stretching out the important parts. Sometimes teachers help children learn how to retell by taking a shared classroom experience and supporting children to retell that experience in sequence. Then, of course, the teacher can help children get started retelling a book that the class has shared.

Teachers need to teach children to retell stories in sequence, skipping over the unimportant parts, and of course it is terribly important to help children begin the complex task of learning to determine sequence. Don't expect that this will be easy to teach, or easy for children to learn, but of course this is no reason to shy away from helping children wrestle with questions such as, "What are the important things that

FIG. 4.2 *A Retelling of a Scene from one of the* Spot *books, by Eric Hill, in the Art Station*

happen in this story?" A teacher will want to help children know that people disagree over what is and is not important in a story, and that it is useful for one reader to look back over a text, marking important parts, and for another reader to do that same work totally independently, and then for these two readers to compare notes, asking, "Why did you think that event was important?" As children do this, the teacher can talk about this question: "How would this story have been different if this part of the story did not happen, or did not happen in this way?" Then, too, there is the question, "Can you explain why you say this scene is especially important to the story?"

For example, Anthony and Sean loved the first scene in *Corduroy* (Freeman 1968). Lisa's mom had told her child that they couldn't afford to buy Corduroy that day. The two boys thought that scene from the book was important—"That happens to me too," they said—and so they built the scene in their block corner, making toy shelves and other items in the toy store, and then they acted out this scene. (See Figure 4.3.)

Before they can plan, partners need to decide who will assume what role, paint what character. It helps children to say why they believe they can especially make that particular character come to life—this reminds them to do so! In the drama station, after a cluster of children had chosen a scene to act out from *The Three Billy Goats Gruff*, Angel said that he wanted to be the littlest billy goat because he has an older brother who takes care of him too. "So I know how the little brother goat will act with his big brother goat," Angel said. The simple act of choosing a character with which one identifies and saying why one identifies with that character will help bring the character to life and can make all the difference in the world. Angel was using his prior experiences to connect and empathize with the character, which leads to deeper comprehension. This is equally important when creating a block structure or a mural on large butcher paper.

Similarly, before children can reenact or represent a story, they need to decide which scene from the story they will

FIG. 4.3 *Anthony and Sean Building the Setting for* Corduroy *in Blocks*

feature. In a minilesson, teachers can guide children to make this choice carefully, with one child proposing one section of a story and reading that section aloud to demonstrate its importance, then talking about reasons why that particular scene is so essential. Then a second child can propose an alternate scene, again reading that passage aloud and providing supporting reasons why it seems especially essential.

Retelling with Detail

Once children have located scenes from stories to reenact or otherwise represent and talked about which characters they identify with before stepping into role, they'll soon be engaged in dramatic and artistic renditions of books. Of course, it will be important for teachers to help children realize that just as written stories can be revised, so, too, children will want to revise their choice time representations of stories. Chances are good, for example, that if children act out a scene, they'll first focus on the comings and goings—the external story. A teacher can suggest children replay the movie and this time really try to bring out the changing feelings that each character is experiencing at the start, in the middle, and at the end of the drama. Then, too, children will probably not think about ways in which their characters can act "in character." The littlest goat in *The Three Billy Goats Gruff* will probably walk across the bridge just about like all the other goats—unless you challenge children to think about acting particularly, uniquely, like their character. This, of course, will lead children to reread, to research, to talk with each other about character traits—and all of that is powerful language work, powerful reading work.

Rereading is an important habit in writing workshop and reading workshop. Teachers might also ask children to refer back to their books to see what other details can be added. When Samuel and Cahle reread *The Three Billy Goats Gruff* (Galdone 1981), they noticed that the troll had a chain around his waist. They were acting out the story in dramatic play, but they used materials in the art station to make the chain.

FIG. 4.4 *Bryanna Painting a Scene from* Spot

Children will often need materials from other stations for their retellings. (See Figure 4.4.)

Retelling with a Focus on Story Elements

It's such a joy to watch children as they retell stories—Juan taking on the roll of the protective big brother billy goat,

Anthony and Sean building the setting for *Corduroy* in the blocks and thoughtfully adding the details that they noticed in the department store. While kids are engaged in this work, teachers can name the story elements for them as they play their way into an understanding of those elements. "That department store you just made for Corduroy—that's the setting of your story. That's what the place is called," a teacher can say. As teachers work with the elements of story, they help children begin to grow into an understanding of them. For example, when *The Three Billy Goats Gruff* story is reset in a city environment, children begin to explore the notion that the setting influences the plot in a story.

Retelling to Better Understand Characters

When we retell our story, we try to make the characters come to life. One way to do this is to have them actually talk, and to talk in ways that sound true, that sound like that character. So the littlest goat will sound different than the big goat, and the troll will sound different than both of them. And each character will sound differently at different times in a story, depending on the character's feelings. When reenacting (and when reading and writing) a story, it helps to be able to hear the characters talk.

When Anna was the troll, she literally bellowed, "Who's that walking over my bridge?" Anna had heard *The Three Billy Goats Gruff* (Galdone 1981) multiple times, had heard her teacher model how the troll would speak, and she demonstrated her understanding of the character with her own voice. How important it is for children to learn to change their voices and actions to match the characters' feelings and intentions.

Retelling to Better Understand Setting

Another way to retell a story in our stations is to re-create the setting to show where our story takes place.

Although children tend to easily understand the concept of characters as a story element, the idea of a setting is more abstract and sometimes difficult to understand. When Anthony and Sean built the shelves of the store where Corduroy lived, the teacher was able to name their work as "building the setting" and talk about the setting as an important element of stories. When dramatizing favorite stories from books, children can name the setting and then think about how they could create it in different stations. When the setting becomes a tangible artifact, the concept is more accessible for an ELL. Figure 4.5 is an example of a minilesson that teaches children to retell with the element of setting.

Retelling to Better Understand Plot

We retell the important parts of our story by making sure to include the problem the character got into and what the character does about it.

Teachers teach this minilesson to help children understand that in stories, something happens to the character. When children are beginning to write personal narrative stories, often nothing happens. They write, "This is me. This is my mom. I love my mom." Sometimes teachers notice children doing the same thing in the stations. They might have

Connection: The teacher holds up the book, *Corduroy*, and says, "Thinkers, you know that *Corduroy*, the book we've been reading aloud, takes place in a department store." She opens up to the page where Lisa and her mom see Corduroy on the toy shelves. "The author, Freeman, helps us to see the toy shelves full of toys." She points to each item as she refers to it. "Knowing the place where the story occurs helps us see where the action happens as we read. Every story maker always puts the story in a place, and the place is called a setting."

The teacher then gestures to a chart, "Ways We Can Retell Our Stories in Our Stations," and points to a sentence that she written just before the lesson: "We can create the setting." The chart has a copy of a page from *Corduroy* with arrows pointing to the features of the setting such as the toy shelves. "Whenever you write or read stories or remember stories or act out stories, always think, 'What is the place—the setting—like for my story?' Then make that place come to life."

Teach: "Watch me as I try to create the setting of *Corduroy* in blocks." The teacher shows the kids how she picks a page in the book that she wants to create and tries to represent it with blocks. "I want to build the part of the story where Corduroy falls off the bed. How can I show the setting; how can I show where the story is taking place?" She refers to the chart as she says this. "Well, I see beds." She points to the beds in the picture. "Let me try to build some beds." She builds some beds with her blocks in front of the children.

FIG. 4.5 *Minilesson That Teaches Children to Retell with the Element of Setting*

"What else would show where the story is taking place? Hmm, I see lamps." She points to the lamps in the picture. "Maybe I'll use the big blocks to make the lamps." She then builds the lamps next to the beds. "Did you see how I looked at the picture and tried to build the setting? I looked for things in the picture that would show where the story was taking place. You can do that in your stations, too."

Using a familiar book as an example in a minilesson is a strong visual scaffold for ELLs, and crystallizing the lesson in a phrase on a chart also scaffolds comprehension for ELLs.

Active Engagement: "Let's all imagine that we are in the block station and we are going to try to build the setting of *The Three Billy Goats Gruff.* What would you build to show where the story is taking place? Look at the different things in the picture." She then holds up the page that shows a goat crossing over the bridge to get to the meadow on the other side. "Right now, pretend you have make-believe blocks in front of you and start making the setting for this story (just pretending)."

Link: "So, thinkers, remember that whenever you read or write stories, whenever you remember or retell or act out or paint stories, it helps to think, 'What is the place—the setting—like for my story?' And remember, you can do as we did, and look in the pictures for help knowing about the setting. Then you can use whatever you have—paints, blocks, actions, your mind—to recreate the setting."

FIG. 4.5 *Continued*

created a scene, but then when asked about it, they will often say, "These are the goats. This is the bridge." In this minilesson, teachers show students that one way to make something happen in their stories is to include the problem the character gets into and what the character does about it.

Retelling in Multiple Modalities

The final section of the unit gives children the opportunity to recreate one story using several different stations, different modalities. While doing this, children can make other adaptations as well. For example, they can think, "What if the character acted differently—what if the troll was a nice troll? What if the biggest billy goat was a mean brother?" They can imagine, too, that the story could have proceeded differently. What if the bridge broke when the trolls walked across it? What if the troll decided he, too, wanted to eat the lush green grass in the meadow?

Retelling to Imagine Other Possibilities for the Character

After we work on a project for a long time, we can look back and wonder if we can we envision it differently. We can ask ourselves, "What if the character acted differently?"

This is the minilesson described earlier in a conference with Anna, Cahle, Brianna, and Samuel about the troll being kind instead of mean. The teacher used their idea to demonstrate for the other children that what a character thinks, says, and does determines how the story goes.

Retelling to Imagine Other Possibilities for the Ending

When we envision our project in new ways, we can ask ourselves, "If the character acted differently, would the ending be different?"

Once children have practiced changing how the character acts, they soon realize that this may change the ending of the story. Anna, Cahle, Brianna, and Samuel changed the ending of the billy goats story so that the goats ate some grass and played hide-and-seek with the kind troll. This is a powerful minilesson because it encourages kids to consider multiple perspectives.

Retelling in New Forms

When we think about our project, we can ask, "How would it look in another station?"

When a student writes over and over about the same topic (trips to the park are a popular one), teachers may encourage them to revise their writing by using another genre: a poem about the park, an all-about book about the park, and so on. Teaching children to tell their story in another sign system parallels this type of revision. After Sean and Anthony built the setting for *Corduroy* in the block station, the teacher encouraged them to retell the story in the drama station, and then they painted scenes from *Corduroy* in the art station.

Adding to Retelling with Writing

We can ask, "What kind of writing can I do to help the audience understand the story better?"

Teachers can teach kids to add to their projects through different kinds of writing. Students can make labels or signs for a final project or write an explanation or how-to book to teach others how the project was constructed so others can re-create that particular kind of retelling.

Conferences

Conferring will change as the year unfurls. For one thing, children will now be working between texts and the modalities available in their centers, so teacher conferences will encompass reading as well as writing now. Then, too, children should have a growing repertoire of skills and strategies that they can draw upon by now. If a teacher, on Monday, taught children that retelling can involve taking on the voices of characters and if, on Tuesday, the minilesson focused on the importance of characters acting precisely like themselves, then in a conference on Tuesday, the teacher might well refer to the previous lessons encouraging children to take on the voices of characters, only this time that lesson might contain a new overlay: "Just like you want to think about how your character walks, you want to think about how your character talks, too." That is, during conferences, teachers remind children to draw on their cumulative knowledge of all they have learned. Often this means that teachers and children refer to charts of previous days' teaching points—and of course, they refer to charts from the reading workshop and the writing workshop as well as from choice time.

Coaching Conferences

When Jose assumed the role of the peddler from *Caps for Sale* (Slobodkina 1987), he repeated the line "Caps! Caps for sale! Fifty cents a cap!" over and over. He did so with a flat voice. His teacher decided to show Jose that a character's voice needed to match the character's actions and feelings. The peddler was trying to sell caps, so chances are good that his voice would be loud and maybe even melodic. The teacher also showed Jose the exclamation marks in the book and modeled to show what they meant and then reminded Jose that whenever he became a character from a book, his voice needed to match the character's actions and feelings.

If Jose had been in the preproduction/silent stage, his teacher may not have chosen to confer on voice quality. He might, instead, have suggested that a reader can read a page, remember that part of a story, and think, "How is the guy feeling?" and then show the character's feelings on his face. With this child, the teacher might have modeled just minimalistic language, calling "Caps, Caps, caps" and then adding, "Caps for sale, caps for sale."

When coaching children in the early production stage of language acquisition, teachers often ask questions that can be answered by simple vocabulary such as yes or no and who, what, where, and when questions (Chen and Mora-Flores 2006, 9). For example, the teacher might ask, "What is the peddler saying?" Or, "What is he selling?" Or even, "Is he selling those caps?"

Partnership Conferences

Juan and Yesenia were paired because Yesenia was at a slightly higher level of language acquisition than Juan. This helped extend Juan's language because Yesenia could model language that was slightly above what Juan could produce on his own (Gibbons 1993). Yesenia was a great partner for Juan because she also knew to use facial expressions and gestures to make her language comprehensible.

In the block station, Juan and Yesenia worked together cooperatively, but the ideas for the house they were building came mostly from Yesenia. After complimenting the partners on how they were cooperating, the teacher suggested that Juan offer two ideas and Yesenia offer two ideas. The teacher demonstrated how to sketch an idea and then talk about the sketch. The use of sketches gave Juan the opportunity to extend his thinking through a visual scaffold. He pointed to the roof that he wanted to include on the house and said, "Top of house." The teacher then reminded Yesenia and Juan that every time they worked with a partner, it was important to have each partner give ideas and then use the ideas of both partners when they were working. The teacher also reminded them that they could use sketches (and pictures from books) to help them.

This story play unit propels learning and creates opportunities where all kids can take risks and construct meaning from their own experiences (Burke and Short 1991). Every child should have an opportunity to assume an identity by building on his passions, interests, and what he does well. All students with myriad learning strengths and challenges deserve entry to the highest levels of literacy through multiple sign systems, and teachers can ensure success for ELLs.

Teaching Shares

There are endless possibilities for teaching shares in this unit. It's always wise to highlight extraordinary work, and by using drama, art, and construction work, teachers will be able to give those students who are in the beginning stages of language development a chance to shine.

Rereading Before Starting to Retell

Before we start our work, we can reread the book to remind ourselves of the story and the details of the story.

Sometimes children dive right into retelling their favorite stories and then halfway through become stuck because they realize they have been telling the story out of order or have forgotten certain parts. This teaching share highlights how some children were taking a minute to reread their favorite stories before starting their projects. One way to scaffold this teaching share for ELLs is to have a child reenact how he reread the story before starting his work as the teacher names the teaching point. This helps make the language input comprehensible.

Rereading After Retelling

When you think you are done retelling your story, you can go back to the book and see if there are more details to add, or you can retell a new story.

The expectation in this unit is that children spend most of their time retelling. One predictable problem that arises is when students finish retelling a story and then decide to play restaurant or build a fire station. One habit teachers continue to build on from the previous unit is stamina. Therefore, in this share, teachers highlight how some students were able to keep themselves going with their retellings. One way to scaffold this teaching share for ELLs is to make an authentic connection to writing workshop. In writing workshop, many teachers teach their students what to do when they think they are done. They teach them to add more details and then start a new story; see *Launching the Writing Workshop* in Units of Study for Primary Writing (Calkins et al. 2003). A great way to visually scaffold this share is to refer to the actual chart from writing workshop and then demonstrate how to apply the strategies to choice time workshop.

Checking After Retelling

When we are finished with our work, we look at it and make sure it makes sense. If it doesn't, we take out what doesn't belong.

This teaching share arises out of the predictable trouble of children putting materials in their retellings that don't belong, simply because they want to use the materials. For example, Brandon put a telephone on the bridge in his retelling of *The Three Billy Goats Gruff* (Galdone 1981).

Publication

Publication rituals in choice time workshop might include the following:

▶ inviting families to look at artwork, block structures, and dramatizations

▶ inviting members of the school community and other classes to look at artwork, block structures, and dramatizations

▶ setting up an art gallery with artwork from the unit of study

▶ setting up a photo gallery (or book) with photos that document the work

One way or another each teacher will need to create a way for children to share their retold stories with a real-world audience for everyone's enjoyment!

When I (Cheryl) taught kindergartners, many of my children resembled jack-in-the-boxes during writing workshop. They'd no sooner start writing than they'd jump up, announcing they were done. No one jumped up more often than Jocelyn, a five-year-old ELL with an impish smile. Then one day Jocelyn surprised me. During choice time workshop, she had a pile of pictures cut from a magazine and was determined to paste them all over a piece of tagboard, creating a collage. But instead of rushing to glue the pieces, she tried them first one way, laying the pictures out on the page but not gluing them, and then another way. After each new arrangement, she stepped back to scrutinize what she'd done, then pulled in to have another go. Biting her lip, she worked continuously for forty-five minutes, not pausing to even notice that I was watching her in amazement. By the time children needed to clean up, Jocelyn had not yet gotten around to gluing her pictures onto the page. I helped her put the collage aside just as she had arranged it, promising that the next day she could "publish" her collage (glue the pieces). But the next day, Jocelyn said that she was not yet ready to glue. She wanted to make some changes in the arrangement and select some different pieces. By the time Jocelyn glued the pieces to the paper, her collage was an extraordinary masterpiece. And what was truly extraordinary was that my jack-in-the-box had persisted on a single project over the course of three days.

Luckily, I'd seen the power of Jocelyn's work and had taken photos of her concentrating, brow furrowed, head tilted. I brought those photos with me into the writing workshop, and when Jocelyn popped up after five minutes of writing, announcing she was done, I showed her the photos and said, "Jocelyn, look at the way you're thinking about your collage. I can see that your brainpower is turned on high. I'm wondering if you could do the same kind of thinking during writing workshop."

The simplicity of Jocelyn's reply astounded me. She said, "I like to see stuff. Then I can think about it."

In that instant, Jocelyn taught me so much. I realized that Jocelyn's stamina for writing might increase if she could set photos of events in her life in front of her as she wrote. I asked her mom to send in family photos, and Jocelyn pasted these to the front of her writing folder. During writing time, Jocelyn studied the photos and began to write stories from her life.

Jocelyn ultimately became an engaged, purposeful writer. By observing her during choice time workshop, I discovered Jocelyn's strengths, interests, and passions and was able to use them to teach her in ways that showed her the unlimited possibilities of learning. And after all, isn't that why we teach?

WORKS CITED

Professional Books

Burke, Carolyn, and Kathy Short. 1991. *Creating Curriculum.* Portsmouth, NH: Heinemann.

Calkins, Lucy, et al. 2003. *Units of Study for Primary Writing.* 7 vols. Portsmouth, NH: *first*hand, Heinemann.

Cappellini, Mary. 2005. *Balancing Reading and Language Learning.* Portland, ME: Stenhouse.

Chen, Linda, and Eugenia Mora-Flores. 2006. *Balanced Literacy for English Language Learners, K–2.* Portsmouth, NH: Heinemann.

Clay, Marie. 1991. *Becoming Literate: The Construction of Inner Control.* Portsmouth, NH: Heinemann.

Freeman, David, and Yvonne Freeman. 2007. *English Language Learners: The Essential Guide.* New York: Scholastic.

Gibbons, Pauline. 1993. *Learning to Learn in a Second Language.* Portsmouth, NH: Heinemann.

Krashen, Stephen D., and Tracy D. Terrell. 1983. *The Natural Approach: Language Acquisition in the Classroom.* Hayward, CA: Alemany Press.

Piaget, Jean. 1962. *Play, Dreams and Imitation in Childhood*. New York: Norton.

Ray, Katie Wood, and Lester Laminack. 2001. *The Writing Workshop: Working Through the Hard Parts (And They're All Hard Parts)*. Urbana, IL: NCTE.

Rowe, Deborah. 2000. "Bringing Books to Life: The Role of Book-Related Dramatic Play in Young Children's Literacy Learning." In *Play and Literacy in Early Childhood: Research from Multiple Perspectives*, 2d ed., edited by Kathleen Roskos and Jim Christie, 3–25. Mahwah, NJ: Lawrence Erlbaum.

Sulzby, Elizabeth. 1985. "Children's Emergent Reading of Favorite Storybooks: A Developmental Study." *Reading Research Quarterly* 20 (4): 458–81.

Vygotsky, Lev. 1978. *Mind in Society: The Development of Higher Psychological Processes*. Cambridge, MA: Harvard University Press.

Children's Books

Burton, Virginia Lee. 1939. *Mike Mulligan and His Steam Shovel*. New York: Houghton Mifflin.

Clemens, Andrew. 1997. *Big Al*. New York: Aladdin.

Eastman, P. D. 1960. *Are You My Mother?* New York: Random House Books for Young Readers.

Freeman, Don. 1968. *Corduroy*. New York: Viking Juvenile.

Galdone, Paul. 1975. *The Gingerbread Boy*. New York: Clarion.

———. 1981. *The Three Billy Goats Gruff*. New York: Clarion.

Havill, Juanita. 1987. *Jamaica's Find*. New York: Houghton Mifflin.

Keats, Ezra Jack. 1976. *The Snowy Day*. New York: Puffin.

———. 1998. *Peter's Chair*. New York: Viking Juvenile.

Kellogg, Steven. 2002. *The Three Little Pigs*. New York: Harper-Trophy.

Kraus, Robert. 1994. *Leo the Late Bloomer*. New York: Harper-Trophy.

Krauss, Ruth. 1945. *The Carrot Seed*. New York: Harper and Brothers.

Martin, David. 2002. *Piggy and Dad Play: 4 Brand New Readers: Sledding/Play Ball!/Water Balloons/Lemonade for Sale*. Cambridge, MA: Candlewick.

Rey, Margaret. 1973. *Curious George Flies a Kite*. New York: Houghton Mifflin.

Rylant, Cynthia. 1997. *Poppleton*. New York: Blue Sky Press.

Slobodkina, Esphyr. 1987. *Caps for Sale: A Tale of a Peddler, Some Monkeys, and Their Monkey Business*. New York: HarperTrophy.

Ziefert, Harriet. 1995. *The Gingerbread Boy: Level 2* (Easy-to-Read). New York: Puffin.

Zion, Gene. 1976. *Harry the Dirty Dog*. New York: HarperTrophy.

BOOKS RECOMMENDED
BY THE AUTHORS

Cambourne, Brian. 1988. *The Whole Story: Natural Learning and the Acquisition of Literacy in the Classroom.* New York: Scholastic.

Hirsch, Elizabeth. 1984. *The Block Book.* Washington, DC: NAEYC.

Horn, Martha, and Mary Ellen Giacobbe. 2007. *Talking, Drawing, Writing: Lessons for Our Youngest Writers.* Portland, ME: Stenhouse.

Paley, Vivian Gussin. 1997. *The Girl with the Brown Crayon.* Cambridge, MA: Harvard University Press.

Parker, Emilie, and Tess Pardini. 2006. *The Words Came Down: English Language Learners Read, Write, and Talk Across the Curriculum K–2.* Portland, ME: Stenhouse.

Worth, Karen, and Sharon Grollman. 2003. *Worms, Shadows, and Whirlpools: Science in the Early Childhood Classroom.* Portsmouth, NH: Heinemann.